Heidi L. Schlatter

Heidi V. Patton

Merlin

The Cat Who Thought He Wasn't

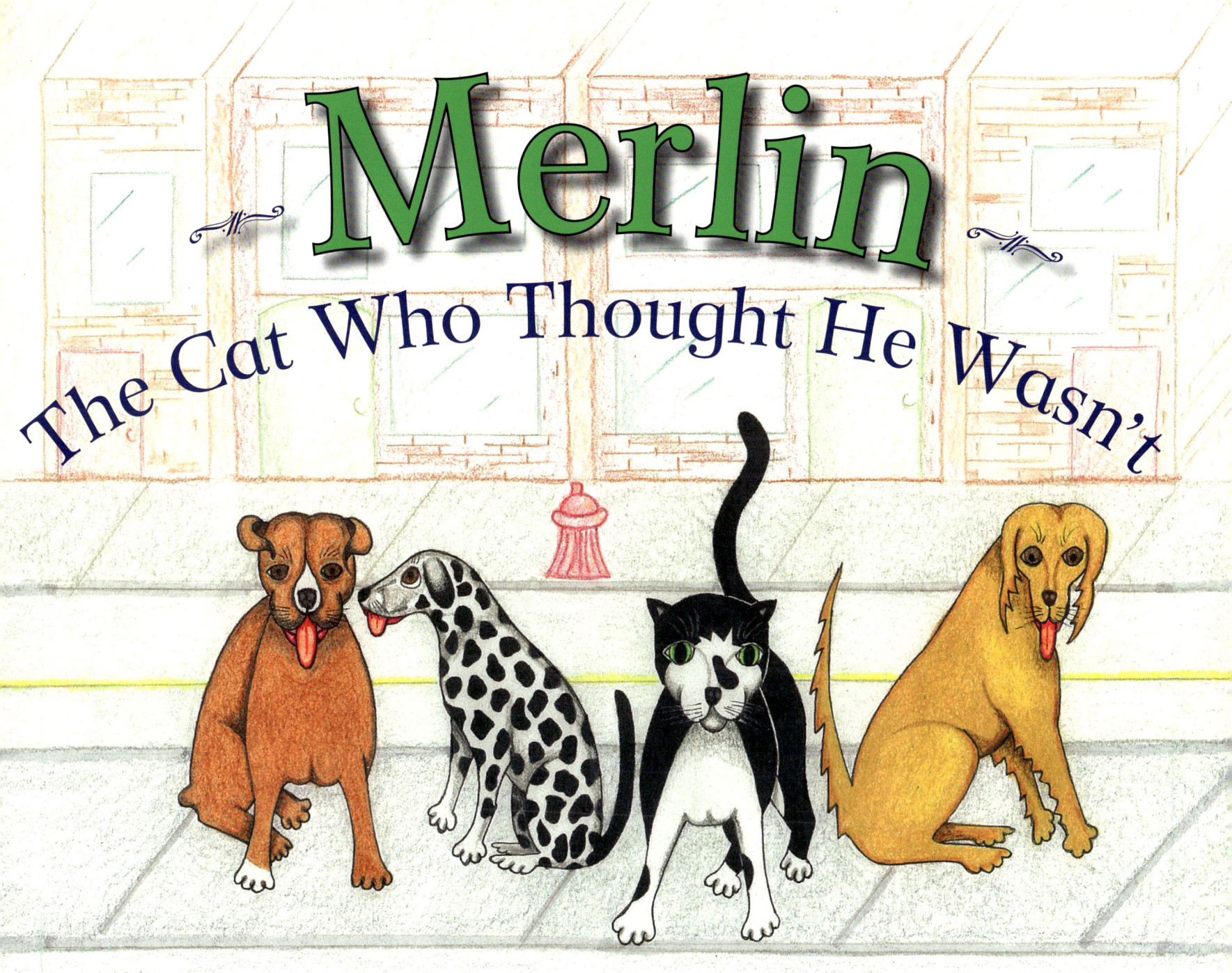

Written by **Heidi L. Schlatter**　　Illustrated by **Heidi V. Patten**

My first name is Merlin,
And I'm from a big city.

My mom calls me Merly,
And she says I'm her kitty.

I grew up with doggies.
They all taught me how to be.

Dogs are fun and goofy,
But they often picked on me.

I have a new home now,
And I never do go out.

I'm fed, safe, and comfy.
There's no need for me to pout.

Pudge is my cat brother.
To me he's itty-bitty.

I tried hard to show him,
I'm really not a kitty.

I watched Pudgie for months,
Doing flips and on the run.

He seemed almost crazy,
But it surely looked like fun.

We have a tall tower.
Pudge jumps up like he's on air.

I tried and I couldn't,
Which to me did not seem fair.

I watched how he did it.
It truly is a pity.

Things would be
   much better,
If I could be a kitty.

I wanted to do it,
And pushed off hard from the floor.

I tumbled down again,
So I watched Pudgie some more.

He flew up like a bird,
And danced around so pretty.

I never saw such fun.
I want to be a kitty!

I ate all of my food,
So I'd grow bigger and strong.

I wished and I wanted,
It to not take very long.

Then suddenly a day,
When I felt fairly giddy.